Paint Party Business

A **Step-by-Step Guide** on How to Start a **Paint Party Business**

Proven methods by Heidi Easley, Founder of Texas Art and Soul and Paint Party Headquarters

www.texasartandsoul.com

Digital ISBN: 978-1-962656-97-9
Paperback ISBN: 978-1-962656-96-2

Heidi Easley

> " I am so excited that you are ready to start your Paint Party Adventure! I created this guide for the teacher, the artist, the entrepreneur at heart, the dreamer, the crafter, and all others brave enough to spread the love of art with the world.
>
> I also hope your find inspiration in what you are doing and wake up every day ready to serve others. This world is full of abundance and we can create whatever we choose to create. **Dream BIG!** "

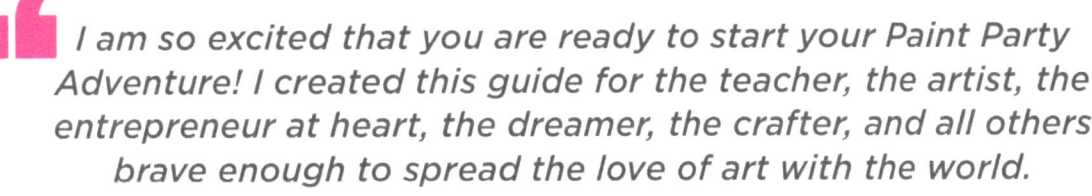

Here's to making the world a more colorful place!

JOIN THE VIP WAIT LIST! This will notify you of all the fun art stuff to come, and when doors open to Paint Party Headquarters again!

So, Why Teach a Paint Party?

Teaching step-by-step paintings may not seem like the "real artist" thing to do, but giving people a safe place to experiment with art can change lives. Paint Parties are not just Paint Parties. Yes, they are a lot of fun, but they also open the door to a creative world that many have not yet walked through.

At first, I thought people would just have a good time, but after hosting Paint Parties for several years, with repeat customers, I have discovered many hidden treasures at these events!

Over the years, I've observed the healing power of art, even in this environment. It has helped the fearful novice artist to jump right in, then leave with confidence. It has allowed a wife to try painting again after losing her husband. It has given people a place of peace who are battling depression or struggling with PTSD.

These are not made up stories. These are all women I've talked to at my events that have shared their stories of how a little painting class can make such a huge difference!

I truly believe art heals. I have witnessed, firsthand, the healing power of art while teaching my Paint Parties. Are you ready for it? I hope so! I am ready to share my advice, experience, ideas, and tricks to help you understand the challenges of teaching Paint Parties.

> We ask ourselves, who am I to be, **gorgeous? galented? brilliant? fabulous?** Actually, who are you not to be?
>
> – Marianne Williamson

Who's Ready?

Buying Your Supplies

Before you go out and spend all of your money on the best art supplies for a Paint Party business, let's first start small. If you haven't taught a Paint Party before, it's a good idea to begin with what I call a **"Guinea Pig Party"**. What exactly is a Guinea Pig Party? It's your very first, very small, Paint Party with friends or family. It will help you get your nerves out and will allow you to get a better feel for what it's like to teach a Paint Party. No pressure. Just have fun!

This first Paint Party will teach you what supplies you'll need. You'll learn how to organize and pace your Paint Party events so everyone ends with a finished painting and a smile on their face. Even you! We're not really in the business of teaching fine art. We're here to create a fun experience for our customers. So, don't stress and definitely don't go out and spend every penny you have on high-end paints, brushes, and easels. Those won't really matter in the end.

When you're just starting out, buy low cost materials so you can make a profit on your very first party. It doesn't have to be perfect at first. Just get started! Once you start making more money, you can begin investing in higher quality supplies.

Supplies

I always watch for the sales and buy in bulk. I like to make a profit at every party, so I really watch my outgoing expenses to make sure this happens. You don't need everything all at once when you are first starting out.

Supplies

Here is where I find most of my Paint Party supplies from brushes to paint, paper towels, baby wipes, paper plates, cups, and even glitter glue. It's totally doable if you buy only what you need for the first few parties. Here are my personal choices for buying supplies. If you find cheaper places, please let me know!

Wal-Mart

- Craft Smart Acrylic Paints
- Paint Brushes, bulk packs
- Paper Towels
- Baby Wipes
- Paper Plates
- Solo Cups
- Plastic Table Cloths, 3-pack
- Paint Brushes, bulk packs

Michaels

- 2 Large Standing Easels (Use a coupon for 40% off.)
- Artist Loft 16x20 Canvases, 5-pack. (Watch for canvas packs to go on sale, use a coupon, and stock up. Use your teacher discount if you have one too.)

Just Remember

Keep it simple. You don't want to overwhelm yourself with too much "stuff" before you even begin. The "stuff" isn't what makes a good Paint Party. It's the experience you bring to your customers and how you make them feel when it's all over.

TEXAS ART & SOUL

It's Time to Find Some Painters

It takes a special person to teach a Paint Party with ease and excitement. Not to mention the skill required to keep painters engaged and attentive. We want to make sure they leave the Paint Party with something they are proud to show their family. However, if you don't have any painters at your Paint Party, this can be hard to do.

For your very first Paint Party, start with your Guinea Pig Paint Party. This can be at your house with a few friends; just to get the hang of it. Then, you could expand to a larger group of friends or even a neighborhood clubhouse, if they will allow you to host a Paint Party at their location. Don't put too much pressure on yourself for your first couple of Paint Parties. You're just trying to get your feet wet and get a feel for what it might be like to teach an event. It can be more fun with a smaller group of people you know.

Once you begin expanding your business, here are some other places to find painters for your events:

- Local Churches for Ladies and Kid Events
- Corporations for Team Building
- Restaurants
- Country Clubs
- Subdivisions with a Clubhouse
- Birthday Parties
- Ladies Night Out Events
- Private Homes
- Holiday Theme Parties

TEXAS ART SOUL

What to Charge for a Paint Party

So, what should you charge? The price you set for your Paint Party can vary depending on your location, the size of your event, the types of parties you're doing, and how expensive your supplies are. I always believe in a profit every party, so don't go out and buy all of the nicest brushes, easels, and aprons just yet. You don't need these things to get started. You just need to start!

Most of my income is generated through restaurants, private home parties, neighborhood clubhouse parties, kids' birthdays, and church events. Paint Parties can be a wonderful community builder.

The amount I charge depends on the amount of people attending the event and their age. Your prices may vary depending on your area and the type of event you are trying to create. For example, ceramic events or large wooden porch signs may warrant a higher price per painter.

Kid Parties, Age 4 to 12:
$25 per child for 6 to 9 people
$20 per child for 10 or more

Adult Parties:
$45 per person for 6 to 9 people
$40 per person for 10 to 14 people
$35 per person for 15 or more people

Subscribe to my YouTube Channel for Fun New Tips

Set the Date

If you are doing two or more Paint Parties per month, I recommend using **Constant Contact**. With **THIS LINK**, you will have exclusive access to the Constant Contact Event Landing Pages for your events. It's a super easy platform to use that allows you to create a special page for your Paint Party event. It also helps you track who has signed up for your events, so if you are doing a Painter's Choice event with multiple painting options, it will help you track which painting each customer has chosen.

Then, instead of adding the PayPal link to your Facebook Event Page, you would just add the link to the Constant Contact Event Landing Page you created. When guests click on the ticket link, they are taken to what looks like an official web page. This will help you look more professional without the expense and headache of creating a website, yet people will feel even more comfortable purchasing tickets from you.

SIGN UP FOR CONSTANT CONTACT

TEXAS ART & SOUL

Creating a Painting

Ask your painters what they would like to paint. Think about what is seasonal and trending right now. It doesn't have to be a difficult or elaborate painting.

Remember, this is Fun Art, not Fine Art and many people are just looking for a fun creative night with their friends.

If it's around the holidays, find some paintings online as a suggestion then, ask your customers to vote on their favorite. Tell them you will paint a new version of the painting they choose. You want to always design your own paintings, so it's not infringing on someone else's work. You are just using this as a starting point to find out what your customers likes.

If you need more designs, don't forget to check out Paint Party Headquarters for rights to a bunch of great on-trend paintings that you can use for your Paint Party events.

JOIN THE VIP WAIT LIST!
This will notify you of all the fun art stuff to come, and when doors open to Paint Party Headquarters again!

For my first event, I taught Starry Night. It's a popular painting and easy to teach. It also has a bunch of little dashes, so it's pretty simple to break down, however you do have to move the painters along during this painting or they will be painting forever.

I try to manage the time and keep my Paint Parties to around two to two and a half hours. Anything longer tends to get stressful for the first-time painter. Once you get the hang of it, design paintings that take you about an hour to duplicate. This should translate to about two and a half hours for the beginner artist.

Stick to the style you know well and create paintings that will ensure success for the beginner artist.

TIP: *Ugly paintings are bad business so, set your customers up for success!*

JOIN THE VIP WAIT LIST!
This will notify you of all the fun art stuff to come, and when doors open to Paint Party Headquarters again!

5 Creating a Flyer

I use **Canva** to make my event flyers. It's an easy and free online program with many great templates and images that you can use for your marketing materials. Just create a flyer with a picture of the painting your customers will be painting that night. Add the event details and include information on how to register for the event. Then, save it as a JPEG so you can share through email and on your Facebook Business Page.

Marketing flyers will help make the event look official and fun. Another tip is to add the words "Beginners Welcome!". This will encourage those with no painting experience and those who may be a bit nervous to sign up too.

CREATE A FREE ACCOUNT ON CANVA

TEXAS ART ♥ SOUL

Need help with Marketing?
Join us inside Paint Party Headquarters.

JOIN THE VIP WAIT LIST!
This will notify you of all the fun art stuff to come, and when the doors open to Paint Party Headquarters

Confirm and Remind

Let's get real...People are busy!

It's your job to remind them of the event and to get people excited.

Nothing is worse than putting a ton of work into something and it fizzles out. It's your job to keep the excitement building about the Paint Party!

I send my event flyer out a month before the Paint Party and say "Save the Date!". You can also offer a $5 discount for any Early Bird Registrations if they register by a certain date.

About two weeks out, send the flyer again with a message about the Paint Party to your invitees. Then, again a week out and again a few days before the scheduled party. This will help you get last minute people to pay in advance and to help ensure attendance.

Also, post event updates, party information, information on how to sign up, and an event date countdown on your Facebook Business Page often. Many people don't sign up until the last week, so don't get discouraged.

7 Paint Day Set Up

Luck Favors the Prepared!

I would rather be prepared than behind. So, I set up EARLY! Yes, many times too early, but I've learned the hard way. Being a little late can turn into a rushed and stressful start to your Paint Party. It's not fun.

You want the party space to feel relaxed and inviting. I usually set up about one and a half hours ahead of time for a party of 15 painters or less. For parties of 15 or more, I'll usually begin setting up two to three hours beforehand.

You want to give yourself time to mingle with your guests when they arrive, instruct them on what they'll need to get ready to paint, and collect their email addresses. This can be done on a sign-up sheet or through a door prize survey.

Taking the time to greet each painter will help them feel welcomed and ready for the Paint Party. And getting your customers' email addresses is a great way to advertise future events. Remember, people come to your Paint Parties because they like YOU and the way you make them feel. You are your business' brand. So, give yourself plenty of time to prepare and set up for the Paint Party. Give yourself time to talk to your guests and make them feel excited for the fun time ahead.

What to Set Up First:

- Plastic Table Cloths
- Canvases
- 2 Brushes, each
- Door Prize Surveys
- Apron on each chair (if you have them)
- Easels (if you have them)
- Paper Towels
- Water Cup, 1/2 filled
- Business Cards (if you have them)
- Teaching Easels with a complete painted version on display

Then, start filling paint plates about 30 minutes before. Sooner, if the party is larger than 15 people.

TEXAS ART SOUL

Need help with Marketing?
Join us inside
Paint Party Headquarters.

JOIN THE VIP WAIT LIST!

This will notify you of all the fun art stuff to come, and when the doors open to Paint Party Headquarters

SURROUND YOURSELF
with the
DREAMERS *and the* DOERS
the BELIEVERS *and* THINKERS

But most of all,

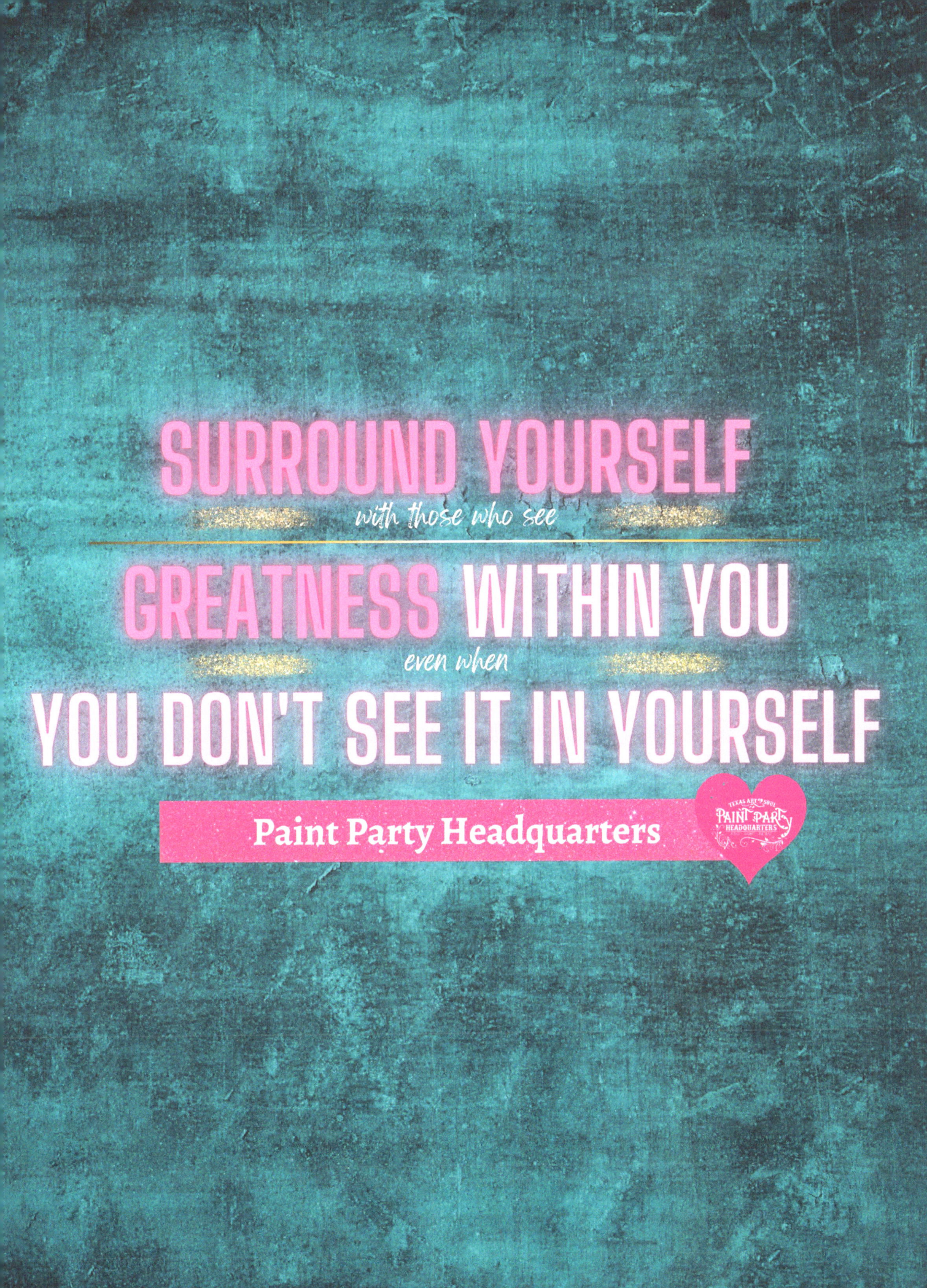

During the Event

During the painting process, walk around the entire time. I circle around my painters like a shark. I talk to them and ask them questions about where they live, their family, and if they have painted before.

Watch how the group is progressing. You'll know when to move to the next step. Just keep it moving forward. Some people can work all night, so you want to be respectful of everyone's time. You will become more familiar and better at pacing your Paint Parties as you go. This part takes practice, but you'll get it.

Give tips throughout. Encourage breaks. If your painters look like they are stressing, say "Don't forget to take a break and look at your neighbors work!". Sometimes staring at the same thing for two hours straight can make your eyes cross! After a walk around, they usually come back and say, "Wow, this is looking great!".

After you have announced the last step, make sure to remind them to sign their work and offer glitter glue. Yes, I said glitter glue! It's so much fun to add to your paintings and glitter makes everything better!

Help When Needed

I help in any way I can. If a person needs help outlining, I always jump in. If I see a painter that is struggling with their wording, I help. If they can't get a painting technique quite right, I help. I love painting and it gives me a break.

Remember, ugly paintings are bad for business, so help however you can. Make sure they feel successful and are having fun.

When I first began my Paint Party business, I used to make tracers for my customers. They could choose to trace the design onto their canvas or draw it themselves. I soon realized that everyone was just using the tracer. So, now I pre-draw the basic outline on each canvas for my customers, before the Paint Party event. They love this! I always keep a few blank canvases ready for the experienced artist in the group who may not want a pre-traced canvas.

Event Photos

Remember to take pictures throughout the process for posting to your social media. Ask people to smile. Photos turn out better with a smile than with a weird concentrated look on everyone's faces. Action shots are great too. You want to be able to tell a story about the types of events you host. You want your social media followers to get excited about your Paint Party events and more enthusiastic about signing up for the next one.

Then, pick a time near the end of the Paint Party to take the group photo. I recommend fifteen to thirty minutes before the end of the event. I let my customers know that they can come back and continue painting after the photo is taken. However, if others are finished painting at this time, they are free to go.

Thank You's

After everyone has posed for the group picture, I make sure to say a quick "Thank You!" to everyone who attended. You have a captive audience, so take advantage of this moment and leave a great impression. I also tell my customers that I will email them the group photo in a few days and, if they forgot to give their email address, they can give it before they leave.

Clean Up

During clean up, first and foremost, my main focus is to wash brushes. This is your most expensive investment, so be sure to take care of your brushes. Dried acrylic paint can ruin a perfectly good brush.

Then, throw away plastic table cloths and trash, but keep the cups. These can be reused. I put all my paint and clean brushes back into plastic totes so they are ready for my next Paint Party.

Sometimes guests will offer to help clean up. I politely say "no", reminding them that it's their time to relax. Once you have an established group, they all seem to pitch in, but I never want my customers to feel like they are coming to my events to work.

Make sure the entire area is clean before you begin packing your car. You want to leave the space just as nice as it was when you arrived. If you leave a mess, the venue or restaurant may not want to have you back. Remember to leave a great impression and treat, not only your painters, but the location, respectfully.

JOIN THE VIP WAIT LIST!
This will notify you of all the fun art stuff to come, and when doors open to Paint Party Headquarters again!

Follow up with your attendees within three days, using the guest list sign-up sheet or door prize surveys. This is where I send them the group photo and thank my painters, again, for attending. This is also a great time to get them excited about future events, even if you don't have anything lined up yet.

Be sure to keep all email addresses in a database. You can use a spreadsheet when you first start, then upgrade to **Constant Contact** as you grow. Constant Contact has a great an on-line email and database system, however you don't need this until you have over 700 emails.

Also, with **THIS LINK**, you'll also have access to Constant Contact landing pages for your events. If you are teaching more than two parties a month, I highly recommend you get Constant Contact.

   SIGN-UP FOR CONSTANT CONTACT

Congratulations You Did It!

You provided a safe place for friends to create and share the love of art! Be sure to post your photos on Facebook and talk about all the fun you had. This will help generate new events in the future and, of course, thank the attendees, again!

TIPS FOR SUCCESS

- You are building a relationship with your customers. Treat them like family! Some of my most loyal repeat customers feel like family.

- Don't stress over the lady who poured all the green paint on her plate while you weren't looking.

- When you are at an event, pretend like your art supplies are their art supplies. Offer different color paints if they want to get a little creative.

- Pre-trace your canvases. This has been very successful at my events because sometimes a blank canvas can stress people out.

- Keep an attitude of gratitude!

- PREPARE! Luck favors the prepared! Have everything ready beforehand, so you're not so nervous and can enjoy the moment.

Paint Party Checklist

- Key for Venue (if needed)
- Table Cloths
- Water Cups
- Paint Brushes
- Paper Towels
- Baby Wipes
- Paper Plates
- Paint
- Guest List
- Email Sign-Up Sheet or Door Prize Surveys
- Easels
- Aprons
- Canvases
- Example Canvas
- Phone Charger
- Music
- Business Cards
- Big 'Ol Smile

JOIN THE VIP WAIT LIST!
This will notify you of all the fun art stuff to come, and when doors open to Paint Party Headquarters again!

PAINT PARTY BUSINESS LIVE

You won't want to miss the next Paint Party Business LIVE Conference! This is a fun event we hold every two years for our Paint Party Headquarter Members and friends! The Painted Prom is always a big hit!!

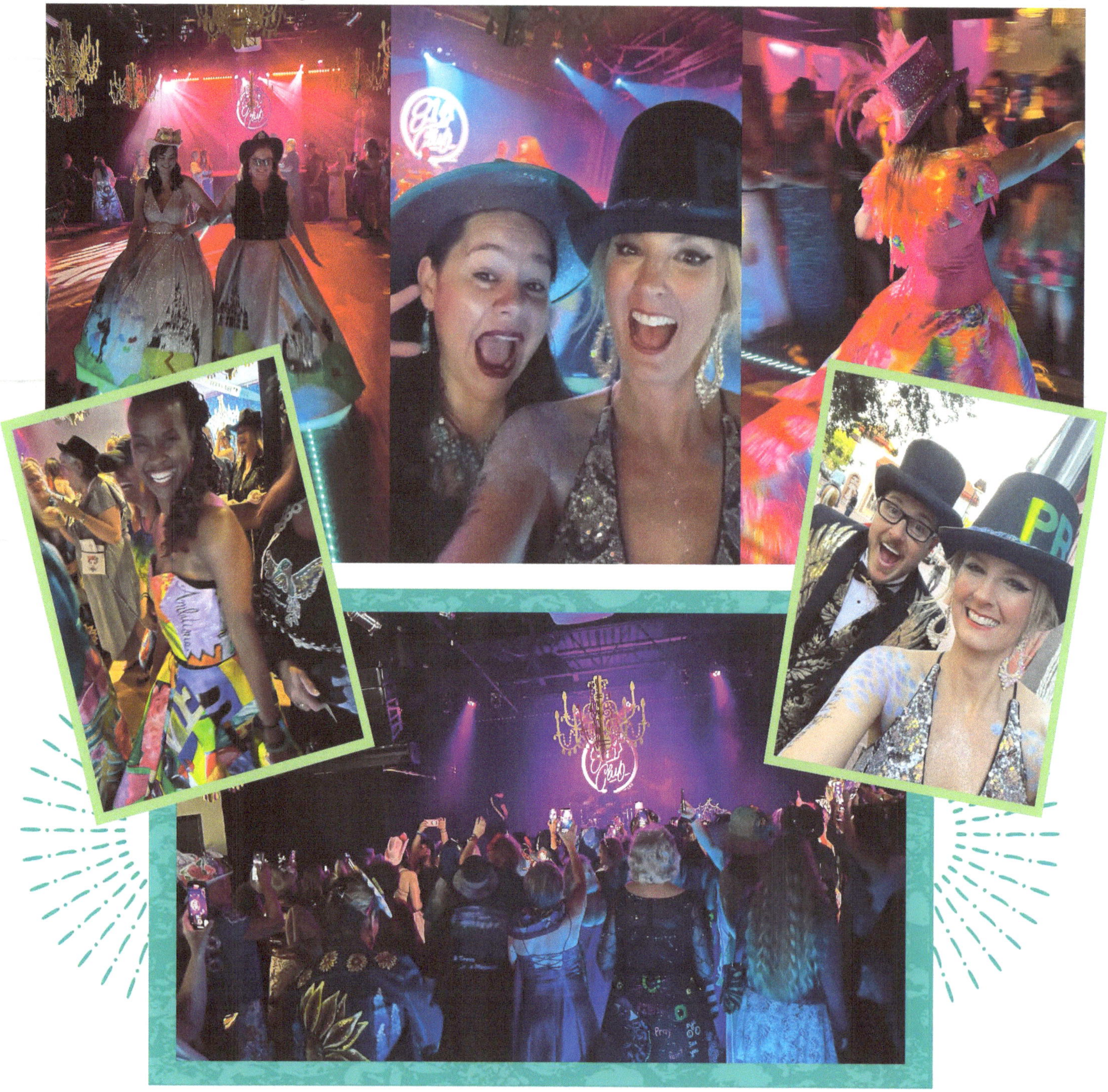

THANK YOU

> *Thank you so much for purchasing my book. I hope you found guidance that will help you along your artistic endeavors and hopefully help you earn extra income while having fun too!*
>
> *Extremely Grateful,*
> *– Heidi Easley*

Want to come along with me to a real Paint Party?

I'll show you HOW to teach a Paint Party! Not sure what to say? How to set up? Or, how to pace a Paint Party event? I'll show you exactly what I do when I teach a Paint Party and give you the FULL Paint Party breakdown! I'll be your personal online mentor and share EXACTLY what I do in my business!

Join the **Paint and Business Bootcamp**

For more programs and mentorship, please contact me:
support@texasartandsoul.com
or visit **www.texasartandsoul.com**

JOIN THE VIP WAIT LIST!
This will notify you of all the fun art stuff to come, and when doors open to Paint Party Headquarters again!

© All Rights Reserved Texas Art & Soul | www.texasartandsoul.com